THE SECRET LIVES OF
MONKS

FROM ATHEISM TO THE
ZOMBIE APOCALYPSE

DAVID WAYWELL

First published 2017 by
Elliott and Thompson Limited
27 John Street, London WC1N 2BX
www.eandtbooks.com

ISBN: 978-1-78396-310-2

Printed in Slovenia by DZS Grafik

TO CREATORS EVERYWHERE
BUT PARTICULARLY THE VOICES THAT
KEPT ME AWAKE THROUGH THE MANY
LONG NIGHTS IT TOOK ME
TO DRAW THIS BOOK:

PENN JILLETTE (*PENN'S SUNDAY SCHOOL*),
ADAM SAVAGE (*STILL UNTITLED*),
RACHEL MADDOW (*TRMS*)
& HARRY SHEARER (*LE SHOW*)

THE VITRUVIAN MONK

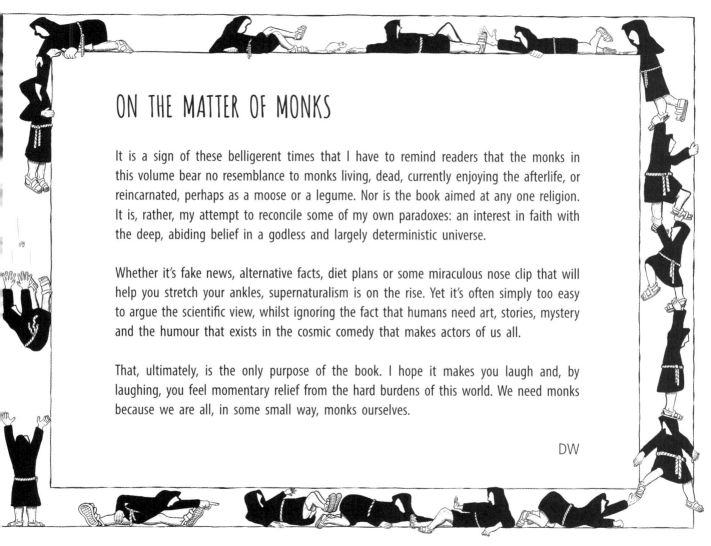

ON THE MATTER OF MONKS

It is a sign of these belligerent times that I have to remind readers that the monks in this volume bear no resemblance to monks living, dead, currently enjoying the afterlife, or reincarnated, perhaps as a moose or a legume. Nor is the book aimed at any one religion. It is, rather, my attempt to reconcile some of my own paradoxes: an interest in faith with the deep, abiding belief in a godless and largely deterministic universe.

Whether it's fake news, alternative facts, diet plans or some miraculous nose clip that will help you stretch your ankles, supernaturalism is on the rise. Yet it's often simply too easy to argue the scientific view, whilst ignoring the fact that humans need art, stories, mystery and the humour that exists in the cosmic comedy that makes actors of us all.

That, ultimately, is the only purpose of the book. I hope it makes you laugh and, by laughing, you feel momentary relief from the hard burdens of this world. We need monks because we are all, in some small way, monks ourselves.

DW

Introduction

What are Monks?

WELCOME TO THE MONASTERY OF SILLY WALKS

NEW MONKS ARE CAREFULLY SELECTED

OTHERS ARE NOT SO CAREFULLY SELECTED

MONKS ARE, LIKE, DEEPLY SPIRITUAL...

MONKS HAVE TO SACRIFICE MATERIAL GOODS

SOME MONKS ARE FUNKY MONKS

BUT MOST ARE JUST PLAIN SEXY

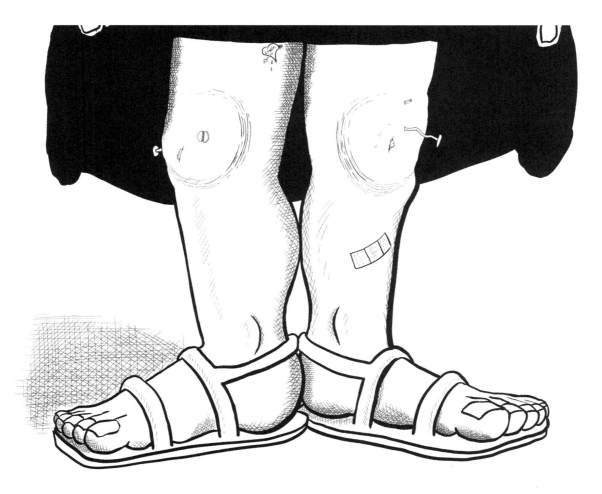

MONKS HAVE KNEES LIKE HARDWOOD DECKING

MONKS IN CARDIGANS ARE CALLED NUNS

THE BROTHERS ARE MASTERS OF CAMOUFLAGE (CAN YOU SPOT ALL 10?)

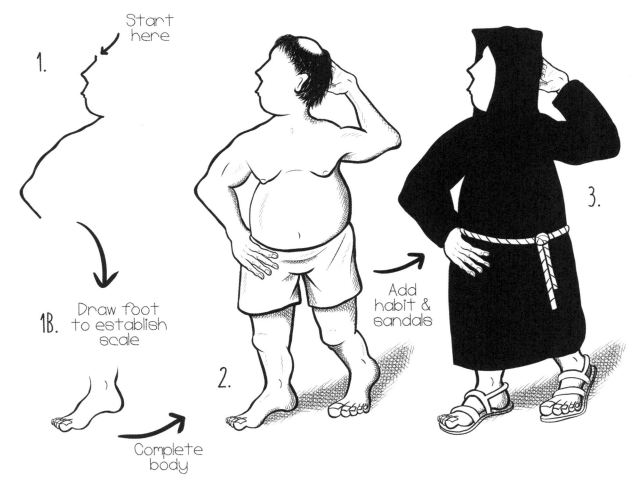

1.

Start here

1B. Draw foot to establish scale

Complete body

2.

Add habit & sandals

3.

HOW TO DRAW A MONK

Book One

A Monk's Day

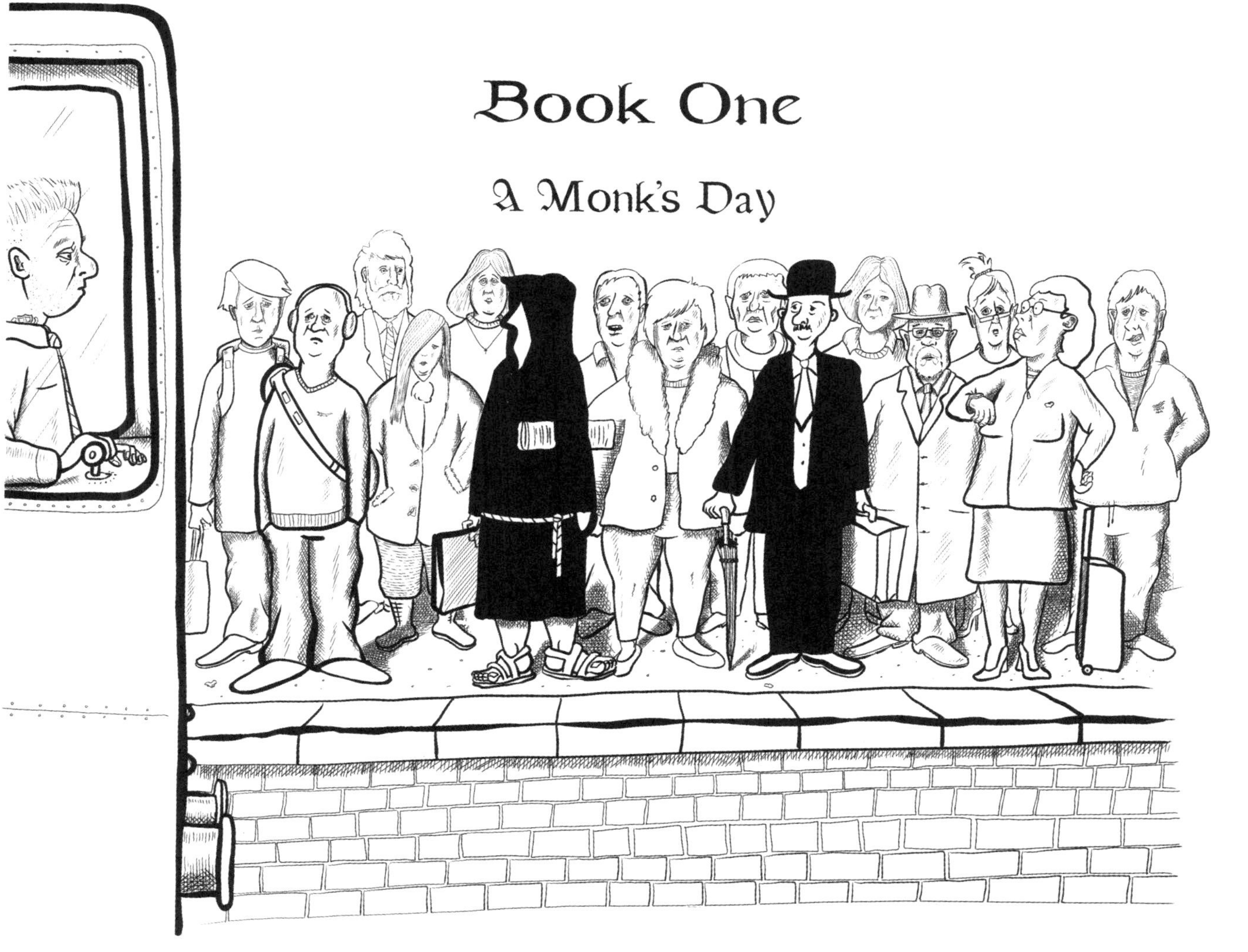

BROTHER LUCAS DECIDED TO HAVE A LIE IN UNTIL 3.30 AM

BROTHER CLARENCE HAD A BELT FOR EVERY OCCASION

ALL MODERN MONASTERIES ARE FITTED WITH LUST SCANNERS

THERE'S NOTHING A POSTMAN FEARS MORE THAN A MONK IN HEAT

BROTHER LUKE COULDN'T BELIEVE
SOME OF THE NONSENSE HE WAS MEANT TO READ

OTHER MONKS WERE IN AWE OF BROTHER HUBERT'S VOW OF CELERY

BROTHER FRANCIS ABOUT TO PREACH TO THE SPARROWS
WITH HIS WOODEN MALLET OF PURITY

BROTHER MORRIS DEVELOPED NEW HYGIENE MEASURES
DURING FLU SEASON

ONE DAY BROTHER STEPHEN SPROUTED WINGS

BROTHER STEPHEN WAS DISAPPOINTED TO LEARN
ABOUT THE DEAD SEAGULL STUCK TO HIS BACK

BROTHER TIM LIKED TO REMIND PEOPLE THAT HE WAS EX-SAS

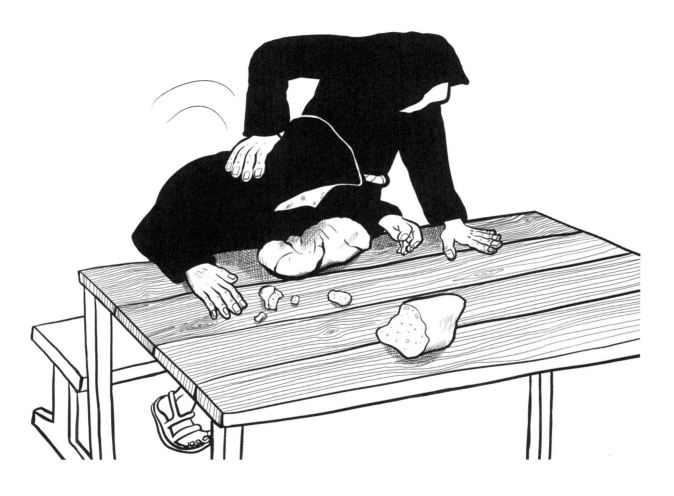

BROTHER TOM ENJOYED BREAKING BREAD WITH OTHER MONKS

BROTHER MARK HAD FINALLY FIGURED OUT A WAY TO MAKE
MILKING THE COW FEEL LESS SINFUL

SO FAR, BROTHER ANDREW'S DEEP-SEA BAPTISMS
HAD A 60% CHANCE OF RECOVERY

HE SAID IT WAS THE COMBINATION OF HAPPINESS AND CLAPPINESS
THAT CAUSED THE SPARK AND SUBSEQUENT EXPLOSION

BROTHER ERIC WAS TESTING HIS RAPPEL GUN TO HEAVEN

BROTHERS MERRIN AND KARRAS WERE HORRIFIED
TO DISCOVER IT WAS A PLAYDATE AND NOT A POSSESSION

BROTHER SAM TOOK A PROACTIVE APPROACH
TO WASHING THE FEET OF THE POOR

BROTHER JERRY ENJOYED SHOWING GUESTS AROUND THE RECTUMORY

DUE TO BROTHER GORDON'S POOR HEARING,
HE ENDED UP GIVING OUT ARMS TO THE POOR

BROTHER BILL HAD RECEIVED A MESSAGE FROM GOD

BROTHER DONALD WAS CRUELLY VICTIMISED
BECAUSE OF HIS ELEPHANT-TUSK HAT

BROTHER WAYNE'S GUN COLLECTION WAS IN CASE OF
APOCALYPSE, DOOMSDAY OR ANY PETTY GRIEVANCE

BROTHER RALPH'S 'BRING OUT YOUR DEAD' BUSINESS
HAD BEEN IN SAD DECLINE SINCE THE 14TH CENTURY

BROTHER BRIAN WAS THE GO-TO-GUY FOR CANDLES

BROTHER HORACE'S FUNGAL TOE INFECTION TOOK A STRANGE TURN

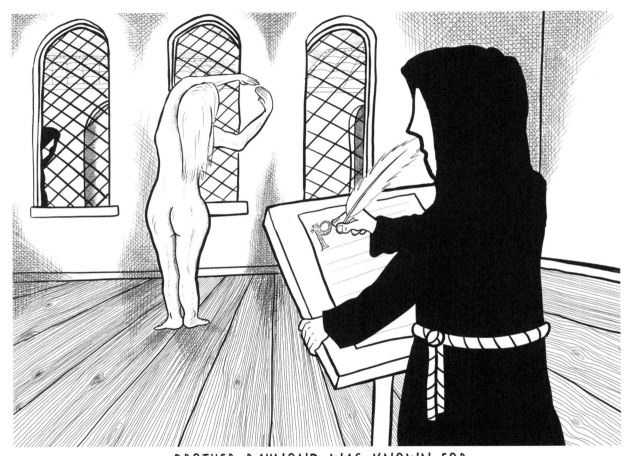

BROTHER RAYMOND WAS KNOWN FOR
HIS UNORTHODOX APPROACH TO CALLIGRAPHY

MONK FACT: THE FIRST LAND SPEED RECORD WAS SET BY BROTHER ALBERT WHO REACHED A SPEED OF 9 MILES AN HOUR RIDING 'GOD'S THUNDERBOLT'

THERE IT WAS: ONE OF LIFE'S GREAT MYSTERIES ON THEIR DOORSTEP

THE DAY BROTHER GEORGE TOOK THE ARK OF THE COVENANT
ONTO ANTIQUES ROADSHOW

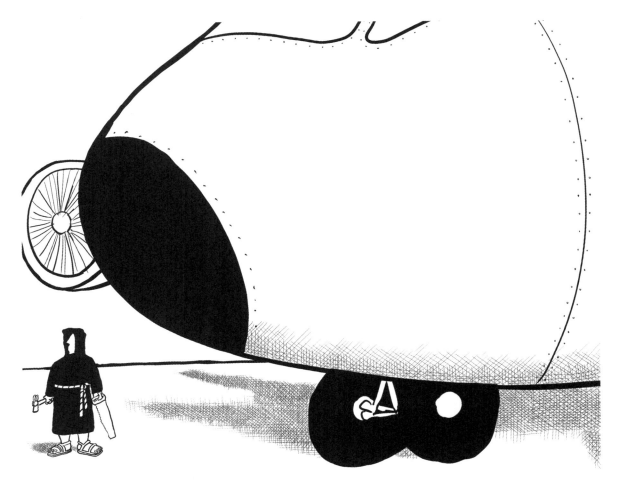

BROTHER OSWALD HAD BUILT HIS OWN FLYING MACHINE

BROTHER CYRIL ONLY BECAME A MONK IN ORDER
TO MAKE ART DOCUMENTARIES FOR THE BBC

IT WAS A SIZE 72 GOTHIC FONT

JUST IN CASE GOD COULDN'T HEAR HIS PRAYERS,
BROTHER RUFUS USED AMPLIFICATION

BROTHER WILFRED HAD A CLAPPER FETISH

THEY SUSPECTED THAT BROTHER OSWALD HAD BEEN
USING THE BAPTISMAL FONT TO MIX WALLPAPER PASTE

IT ANNOYED BROTHER ARNOLD
WHEN PEOPLE QUESTIONED HIS PACIFISM

BROTHER STAN WAS OFTEN BLESSED WITH MYSTICAL VISIONS –
UNFORTUNATELY, THEY WERE OF TRAFFIC CONES IN SLOUGH

BROTHER TIM WENT UNDERCOVER TO SOLVE THE LETTUCE MYSTERY

BROTHER MARK'S STAIRWAY TO HEAVEN HIT ITS FIRST SNAG

BROTHER FRANK REGRETTED USING HOLY WATER IN HIS BATTER MIX

THE LORD STRUCK BROTHER TREVOR DUMB
SO, NATURALLY, HE GOT HIS OWN SHOW ON ITV

THE DAY BROTHER HAROLD DECIDED TO REDESIGN THE CROSS

BROTHER SEAMUS MADE THE RUDIMENTARY ERROR OF ALL NEW TRAPPISTS

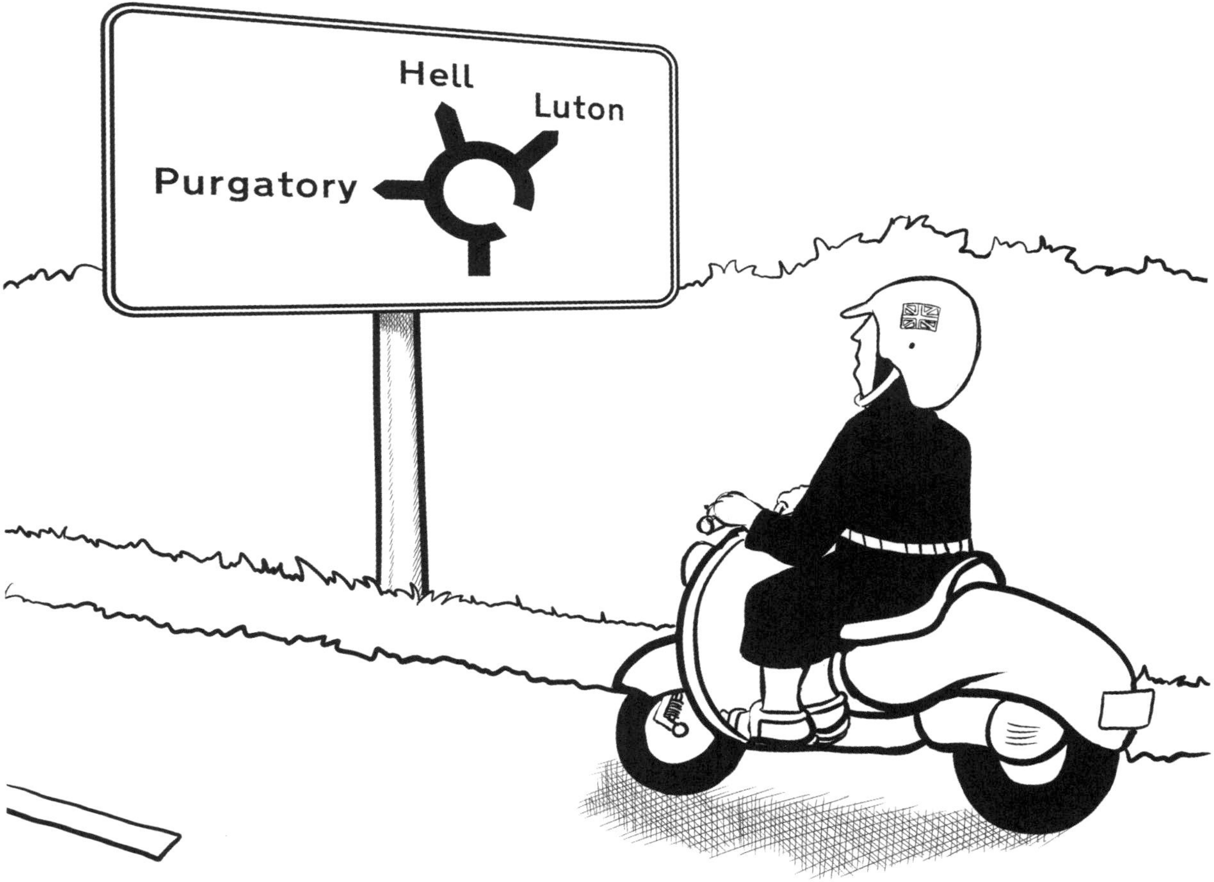
Hell
Luton
Purgatory

AROUND 3 AM, THE BROTHERS WERE AWOKEN
BY THE IMPURE-THOUGHT DETECTOR

FOR EVERY SINFUL THOUGHT, BROTHER RANDOLPH LIT A CANDLE

WHILE THE REST OF THE WORLD SLEEPS, MONKS ARE HATCHING PLANS

BROTHER JOSEPH WAS SURPRISED TO FIND HIMSELF
IN THE TENTH CIRCLE OF HELL WITH PERFUME SELLERS

BROTHER STEWART'S AUDIENCE WITH HIS GRACE
DID NOT TURN OUT AS HE'D EXPECTED

THERE WAS SOMETHING SUSPICIOUS ABOUT BROTHER DAN'S BEHAVIOUR

THERE'S NOTHING LIKE A PLAGUE TO MAKE MONKS POPULAR AGAIN

BROTHER VINCE REALISED IT WAS A SIGN FROM GOD
THAT HE HAD SEEN EXACTLY ZERO MIRACLES IN HIS LIFETIME

THE FIRST THEY KNEW OF THE DEMOLITION ORDER
WAS WHEN BROTHER SIMON CAME RUSHING INTO THE ROOM

Book Two
The Spiritual Life

BROTHER RUPERT DIDN'T DOUBT HIS RELIGION,
HE JUST DOUBTED THE OTHER 4,599 RELIGIONS IN THE WORLD

BROTHER TOBY JUST LOST IT WHEN HE DISCOVERED
THE OLD MAN WAS A BLIND WATCHMAKER

BROTHER ROGER TURNING WATER INTO HOLY WATER

BROTHER HECTOR HARD AT WORK ON HIS 1:10,000 SCALE MODEL OF GOD'S LITTLE TOE

THE PROCESSION OF THE TRUSS OF ST RUPERT

GOD DOESN'T PLAY DICE, HE PLAYS CONKERS

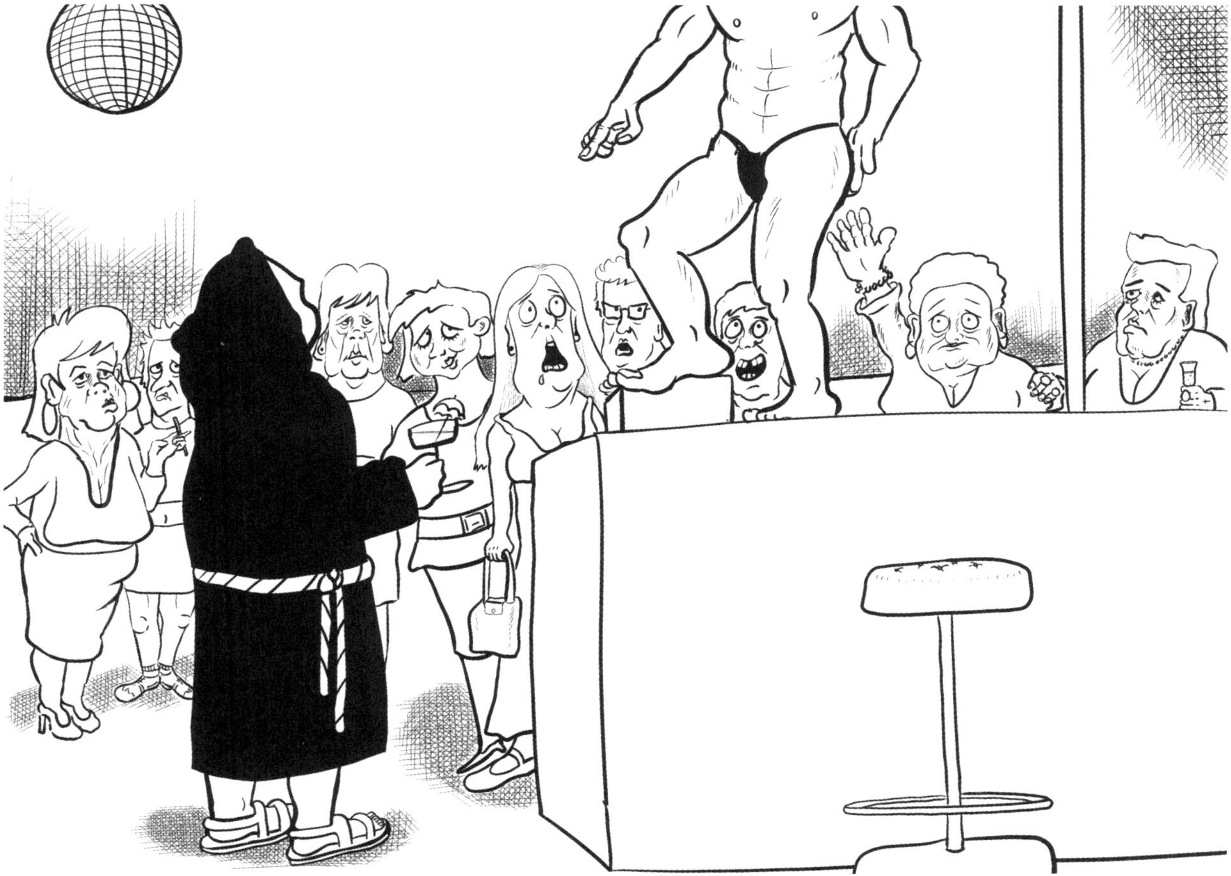

BROTHER JEREMY BEGAN TO SUSPECT HE WASN'T IN THE MISSION OF THE IMMACULATE CONCEPTION

BROTHER RENÉ CALLED IT PRACTICAL THEOLOGY –
IT INVOLVED PULLING A CAMEL THROUGH THE EYE OF A NEEDLE

GOD SPOKE THROUGH BROTHER BARNABY
BUT ONLY IN ANNOYING CLICHÉS

NOBODY COULD EXPLAIN THE MYSTERIOUS 'HELLO, ANYBODY THERE?
I'VE FALLEN DOWN THE WELL' NOISES THEY KEPT HEARING...

BROTHER WINSTON COULD TALK TO THE ANIMALS — UNFORTUNATELY, THEY DIDN'T HAVE THE SLIGHTEST IDEA OF WHAT HE WAS SAYING

BROTHER HANNIBAL WAS SEEKING MAN'S SPIRITUAL ESSENCE

BROTHERS LARRY AND LOU WERE JOINED AT THE HIP
BUT DIVIDED ON THE SUBJECT OF PREDESTINATION

THE CORNER WAS A NOTORIOUS PICK-UP SPOT FOR MONKS

PERHAPS IT HAD BEEN A MISTAKE TO BUILD THE NURSERY
ON AN ANCIENT MONK BURIAL GROUND...

BROTHER LIONEL HAD MASTERED LEVITATION
BUT COULD NOT OVERCOME SLACK UNDERWEAR

BROTHER GREGORY AND THE TRANSUBSTANTIATION OF THE WINO

BROTHER THOMAS DUTIFULLY CATALOGUED
THE ABBEY'S LIBRARY INTO FICTION AND NON-FACT

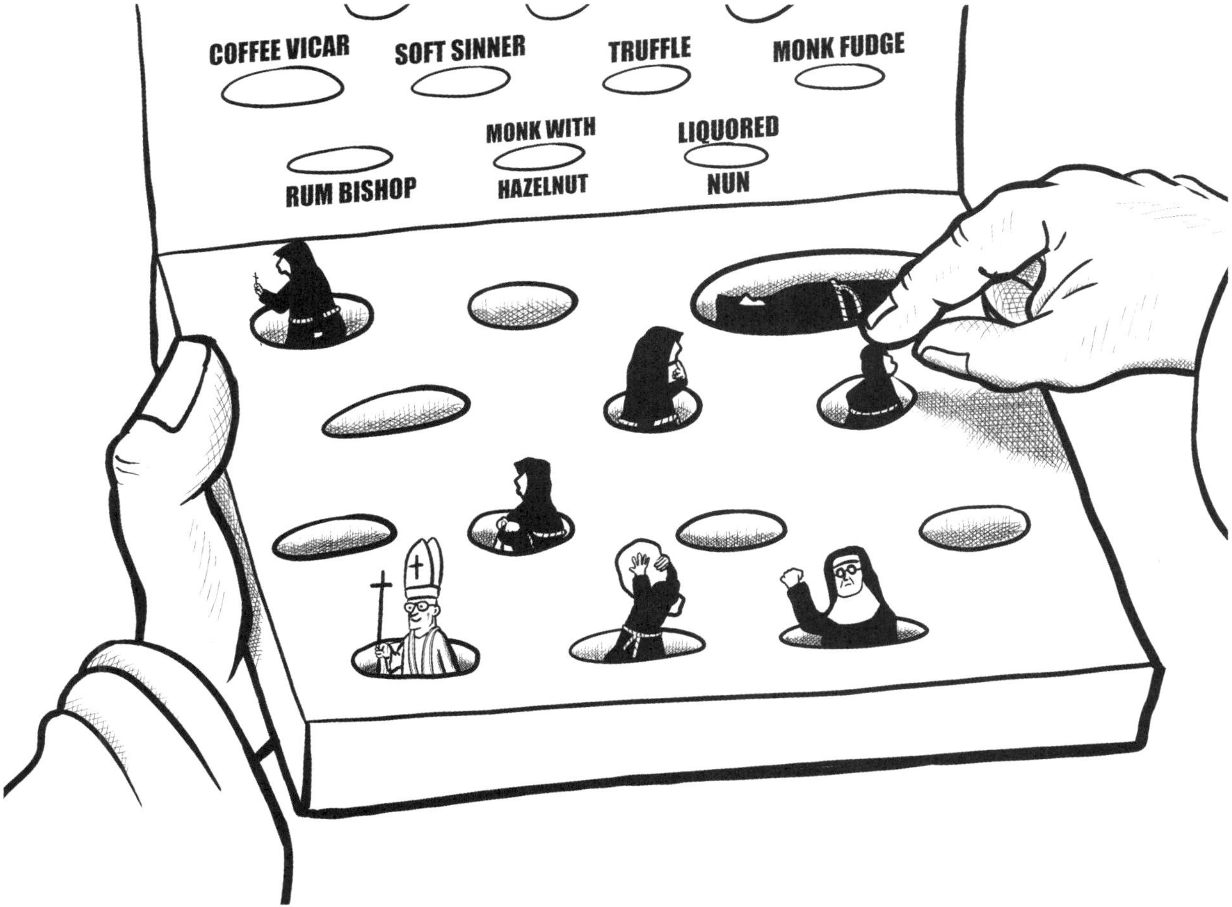
COFFEE VICAR
SOFT SINNER
TRUFFLE
MONK FUDGE
MONK WITH
HAZELNUT
LIQUORED
NUN
RUM BISHOP

GOD'S CHOCOLATE BOX

IT WAS A CONFIRMED MIRACLE WHEN THE
IMMERSION HEATER STARTED TO WEEP TEARS

BROTHER RON HAD AN OUT-OF-BODY EXPERIENCE;
SADLY, IT WAS ONE OF STANDING ON A PLUG

BROTHER NORMAN CONSIDERED THE BURNING BUSH MYTH
WELL AND TRULY BUSTED

BROTHER WILSON DID NOT MISS FEMALE COMPANIONSHIP
THANKS TO PRAYER, MEDITATION AND SWEDISH EROTICA

SCRIPTURALLY IT MADE COMPLETE SENSE

BROTHER MAURICE LIKED TO REMIND PEOPLE
THAT HE WAS CHOSEN BY GOD

AND SO THE CASE OF THE DISAPPEARING FRIAR WAS FINALLY SOLVED...

THE HOLY FESTIVAL OF LEANT

THE JACUZZI WAS ATTRACTING A DIFFERENT CLASS OF BAPTISM

BROTHER BARTHOLOMEW SUSPECTED AN ADMINISTRATIVE ERROR

FOR EVERY INN HAUNTED BY A MAD MONK THERE'S
A MONASTERY HAUNTED BY A POTTY PUB LANDLORD

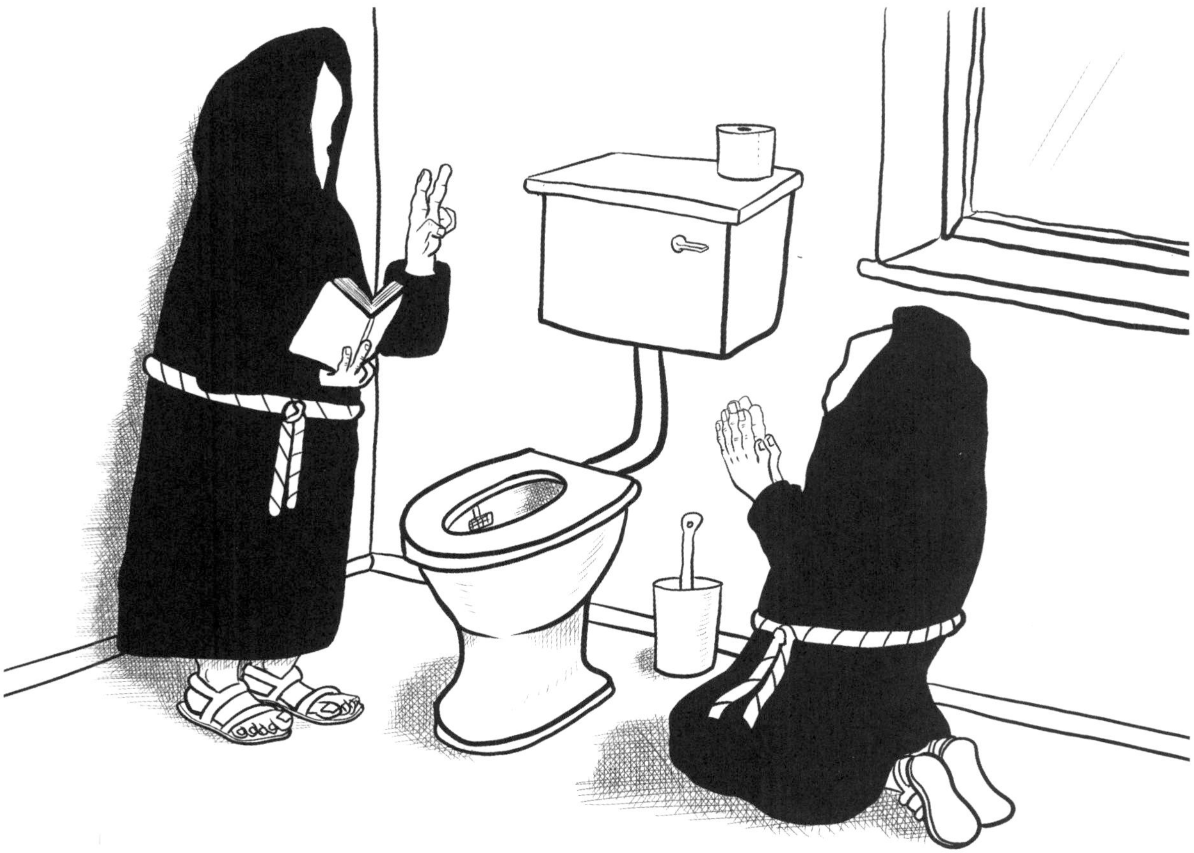

CISTERNCIANS

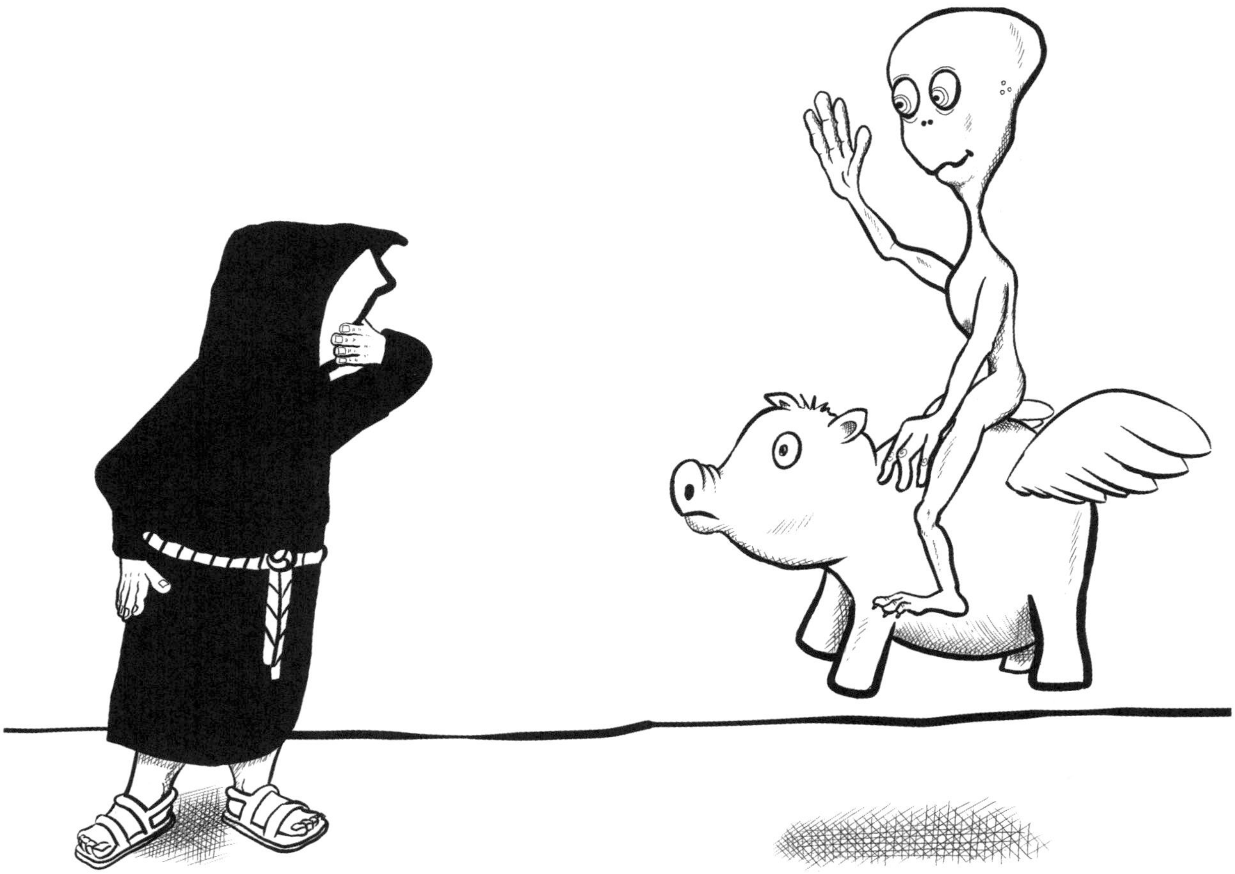

BROTHER PAUL THOUGHT IT STRANGE THAT MIRACLES
ONLY HAPPENED WHEN HE DIDN'T HAVE HIS CAMERA

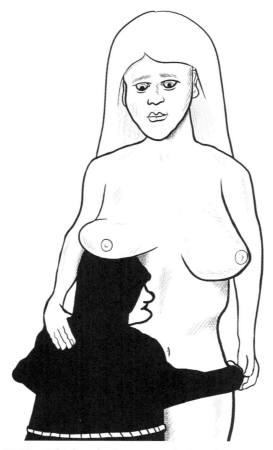

BROTHER TOM WAS THE WISE OLD HERMIT
WHO LIVED UNDERNEATH PENELOPE'S RIGHT BREAST

THEY THOUGHT BROTHER ANGUS WAS POSSESSED
BUT IT TURNED OUT TO BE GAS

SOME SAID IT WAS ABOUT THE MEDITATION,
OTHERS, THE PLEASURE OF A ROCKY POINT

THE DAY THAT BROTHER ERIC, A FUNDAMENTALIST CAMPANOLOGIST,
WENT ON A BELL-RINGING SPREE...

BROTHER WILFRED STARTED TO SPEAK IN TONGUES;
VERY BORING TONGUES...

THEY CELEBRATED AS BROTHER AMBROSE
ENTERED HIS 197TH YEAR OF MEDITATION

BROTHER BERNARD THOUGHT THE SECOND COMING
WASN'T AS GOOD AS THE FIRST

Book Three

Sports and Recreation

AFTER A HARD DAY, BROTHERS SIMON AND ANDREW
LIKED TO PLAY ONION CROQUET

BROTHER LUKE BEAT THE PREVIOUS RECORD FOR SIN CHUCKING
WHEN HE THREW HIS LUST TWENTY-SEVEN FEET

BROTHER BENEDICT CONSIDERED STRIPTEASE
A HOBBY AND NOT A PROFESSION

BROTHER DOMINIC EXPERIENCED THE FUN KIND OF POSSESSION

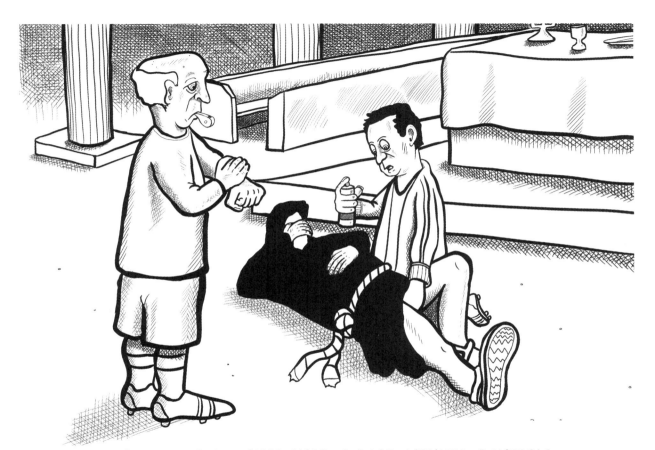

BROTHER RUPERT WENT INTO A LAST-MINUTE CANTICLE
WHEN HE FELT HIS GROIN GO

BROTHER EWAN'S SELF-FLAGELLATION WAS NOT GOING WELL

BROTHER GILES EXPERIENCED A KUMBAYA-INDUCED RAGE

EVEN WHEN IT CAME TO GROWING BONSAI,
BROTHER WILLIAM STRUGGLED WITH HUMILITY

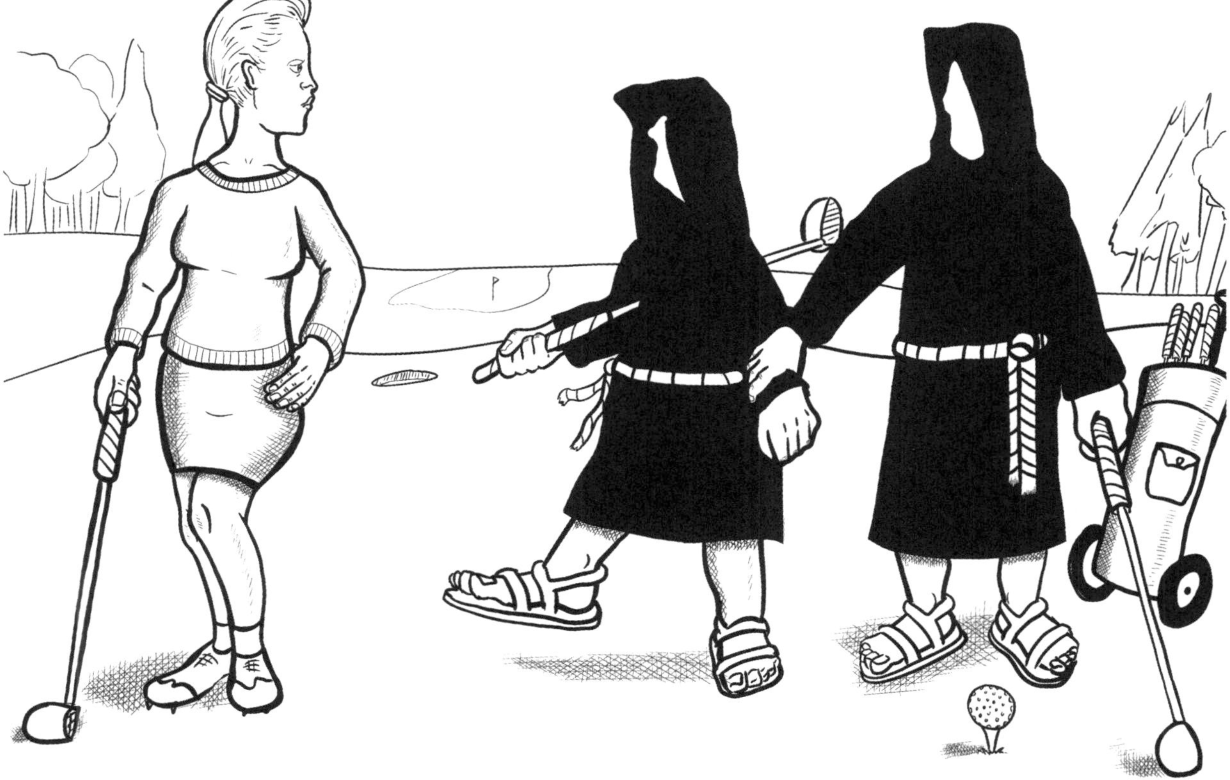

PRO-CELIBACY GOLF

AT CAMP THEY LIKED TO PLAY 'WHAT'S MY PSALM?'

BROTHER JETHRO HAD SOLEMNLY KEPT HIS VOW OF BIGAMY

BROTHER BORIS'S NIPPLE RINGS WERE FASHIONABLE YET GOTHIC

BROTHER MATTHEW HAD HOPED
THAT HIS NEW TOUPEE WASN'T THAT NOTICEABLE

BROTHER AMBROSE HATED IT WHEN PEOPLE SLAM DUNKED HIS HALO

MONK CRICKET ENSURED THERE WAS ALWAYS
PLENTY OF TIME LEFT FOR PRAYERS

BACH'S SANCTUS FOR SIX VOCAL PARTS AND A LEAF BLOWER

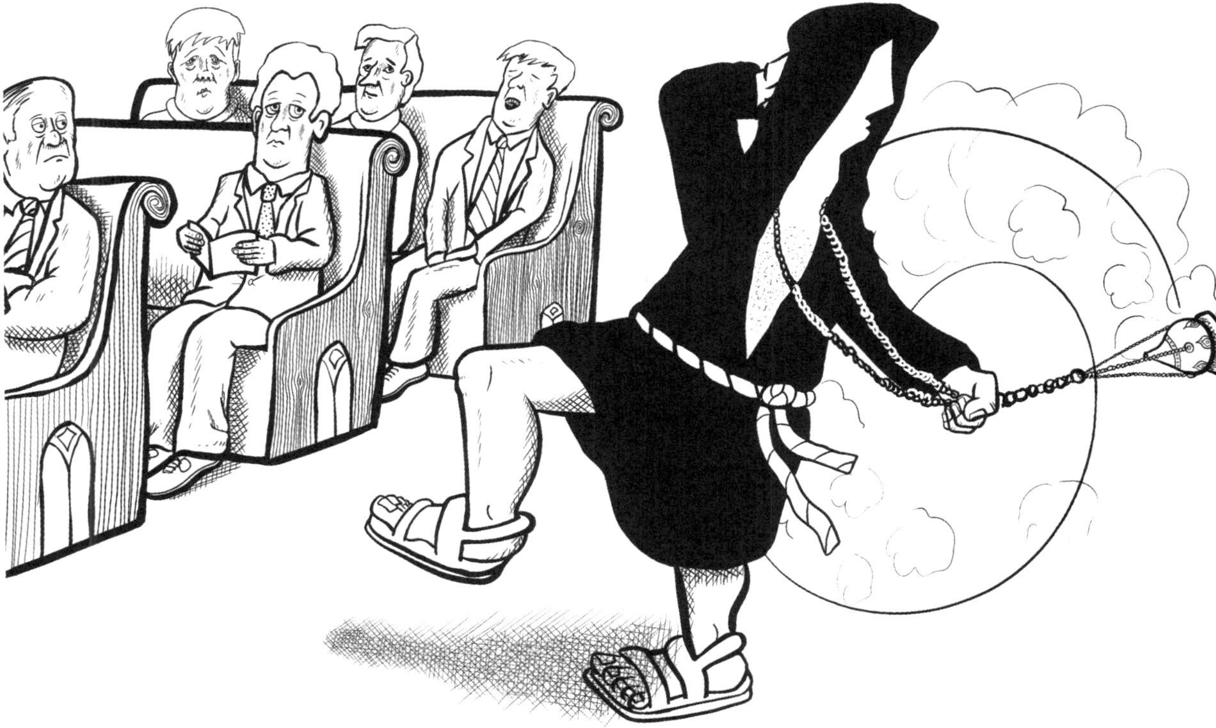

SHOWBIZ!

BROTHER OTTO WAS RAPIDLY
RUNNING OUT OF SPACE IN HIS BEE GRAVEYARD

ANOTHER LIFE LOST TO HONEY

IT WAS THEIR PRINCIPAL VICE

THIS YEAR THE BAR HAD BEEN SET AT A RATHER DAUNTING 'PIOUS'

THE NEW VR MONK GAME EVEN MANAGED
TO CAPTURE THE IMMENSE TEDIUM AND KNEE PAIN

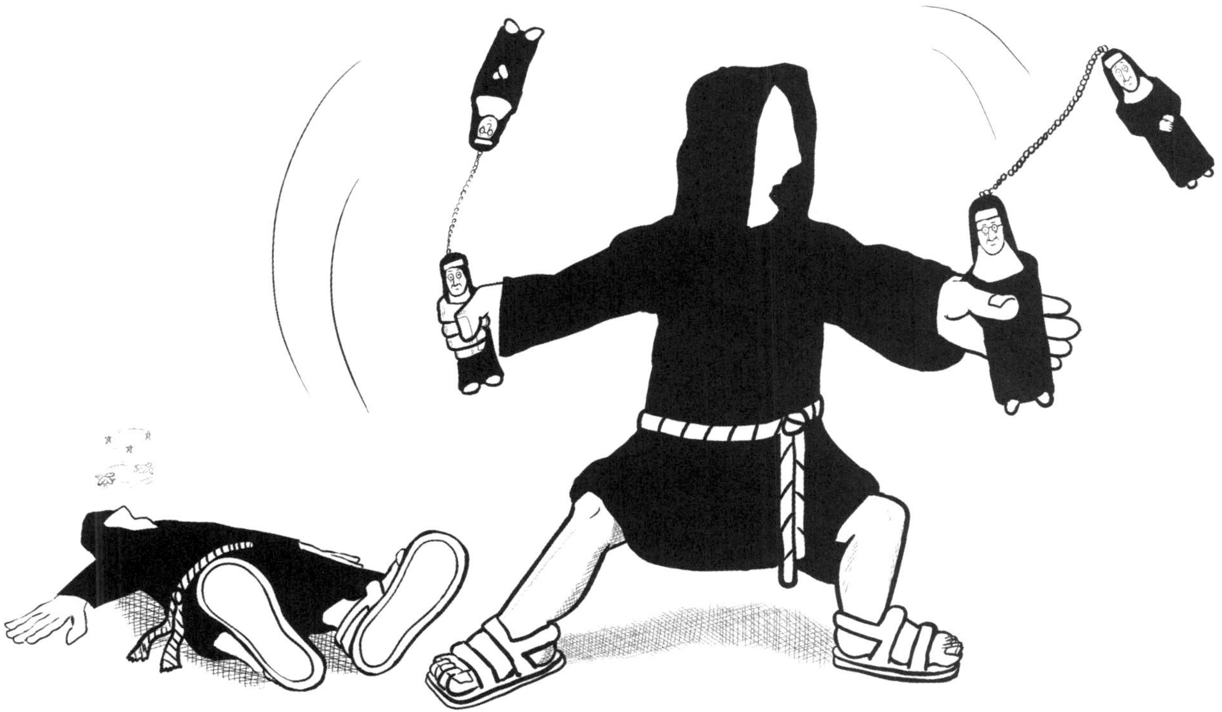

NUNCHUCKS

MONKS INVENTED SOCIAL MEDIA IN THE 15TH CENTURY

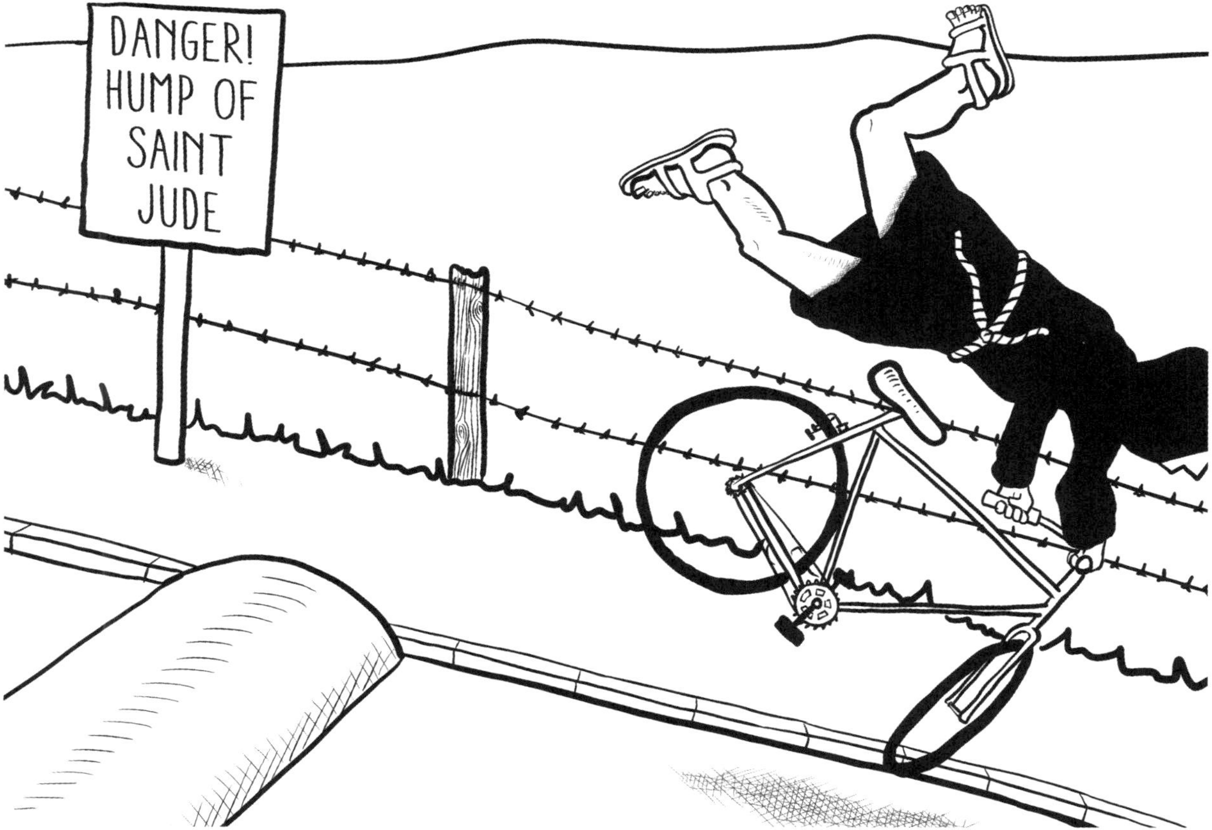
DANGER!
HUMP OF
SAINT
JUDE

FUN FACT: UNTIL 1873, THE SPORT OF MONK TIPPING
WAS BOTH POPULAR AND LEGAL

BROTHER CLARENCE WAS READING AT A SNAIL'S PACE

Book Four

Notable Monks

THE SPICE MONKS: BROTHERS SPORTY, GINGER, BABY, POSH AND REG

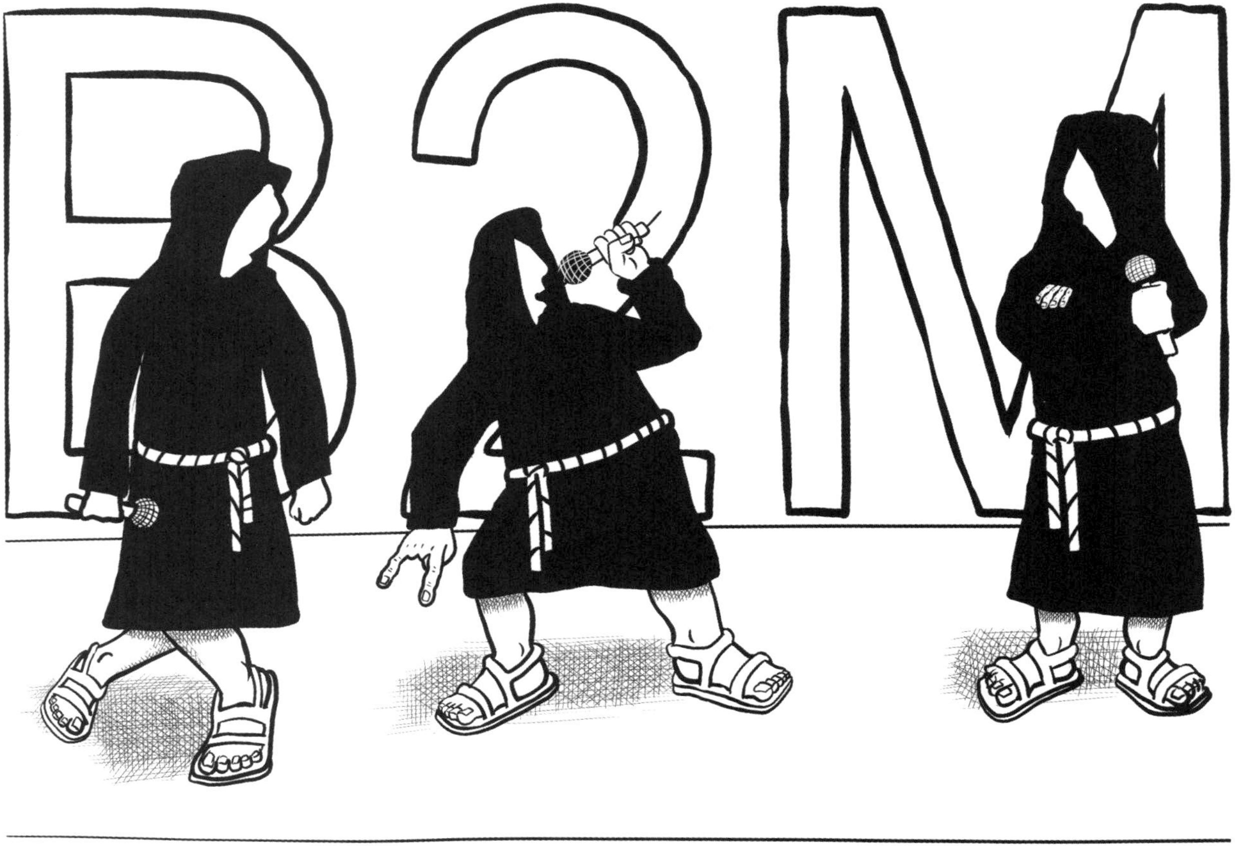
B2M

BOYZ 2 MONKZ

HABITAT

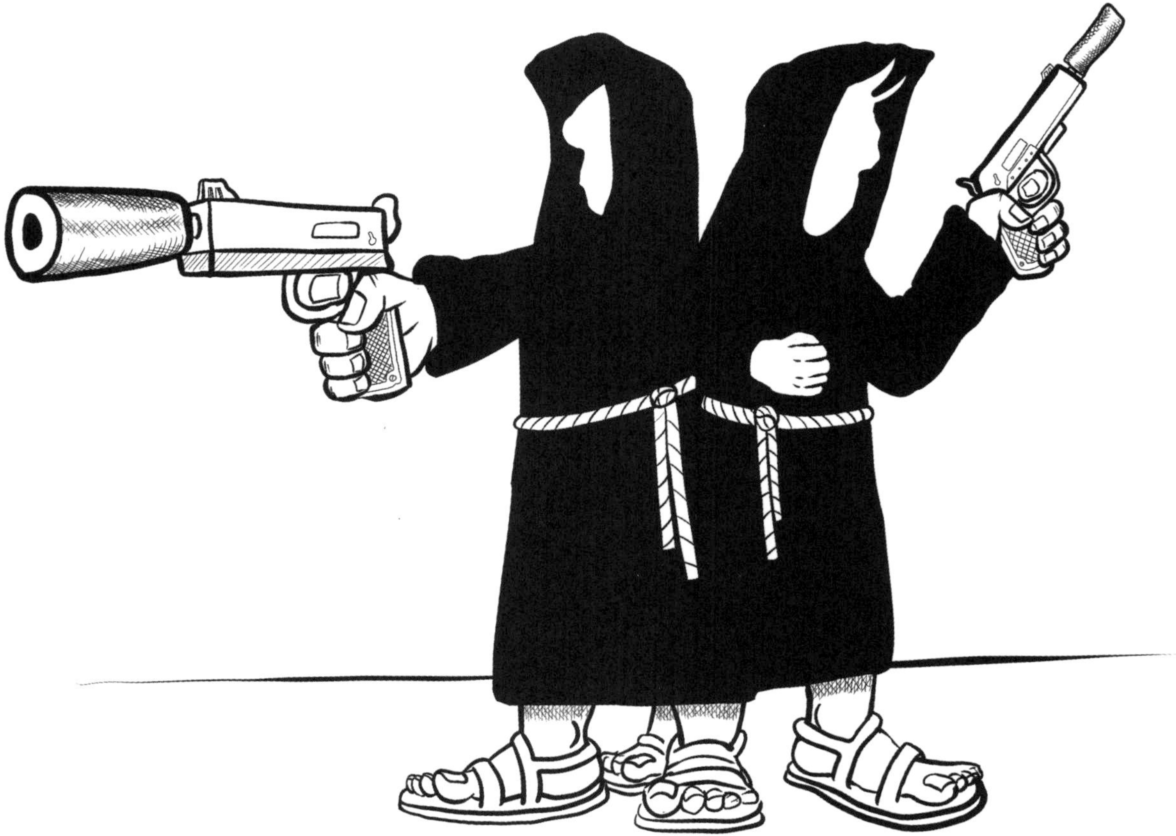

THE MAN FROM MONKLE

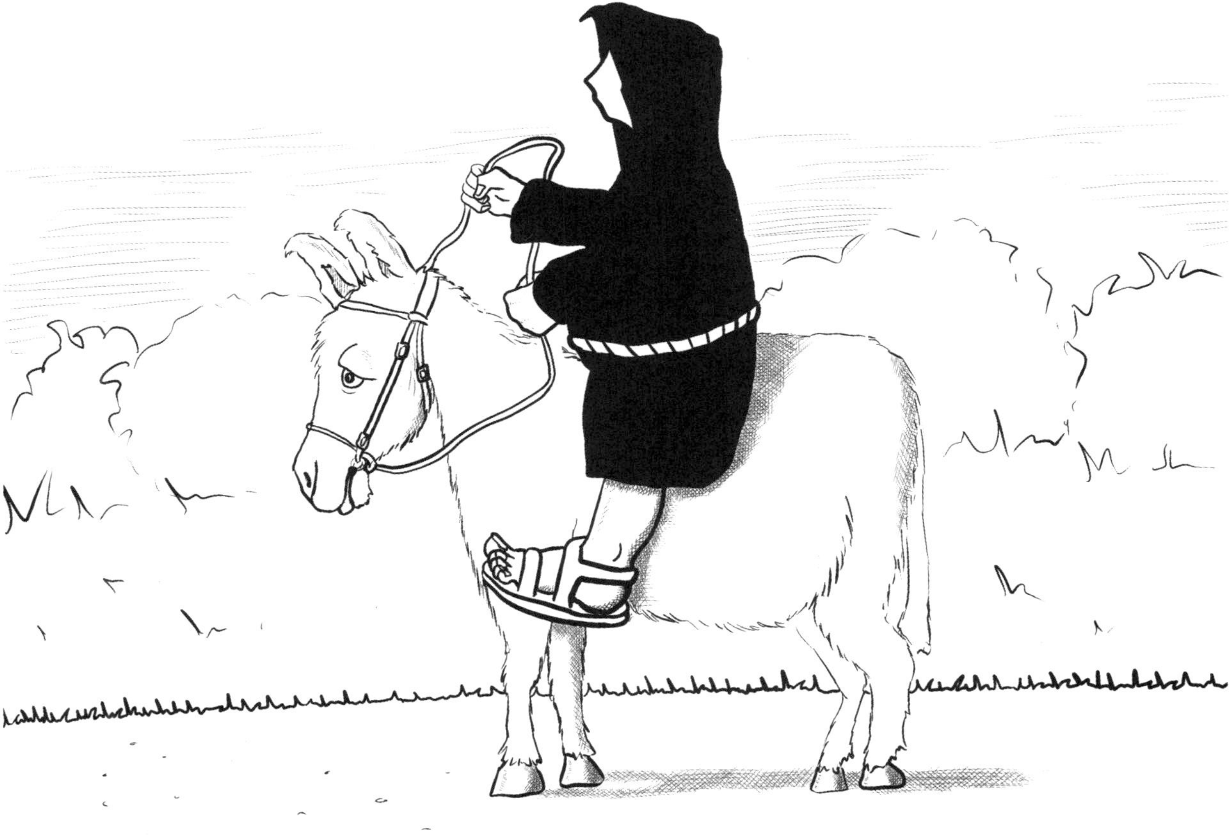

A MONKEY

BROTHER OLAF THE SWEDISH MONK

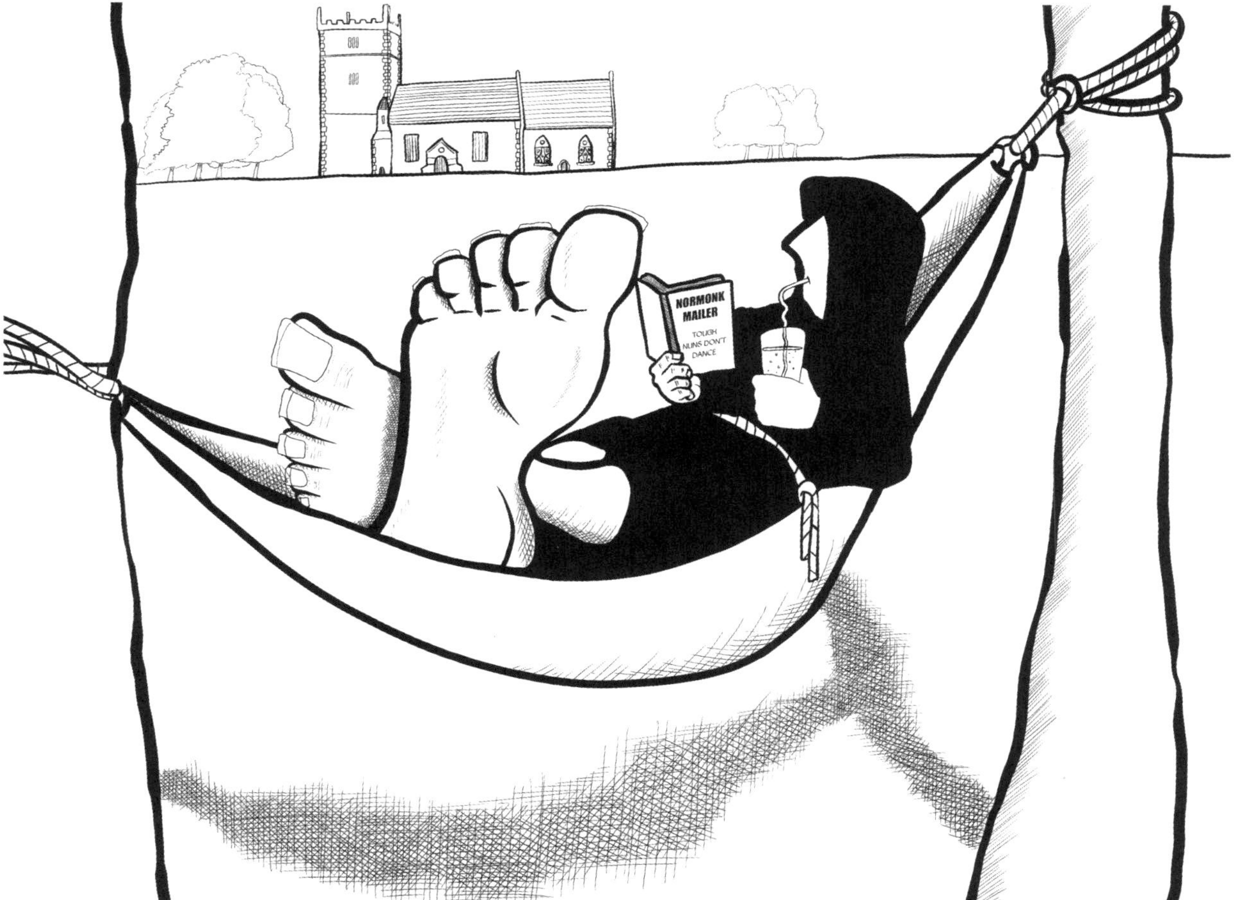
NORMONK
MAILER
TOUGH
NUNS DON'T
DANCE

A HAMMONK

THE STREETS OF SAN FRANCISCAN

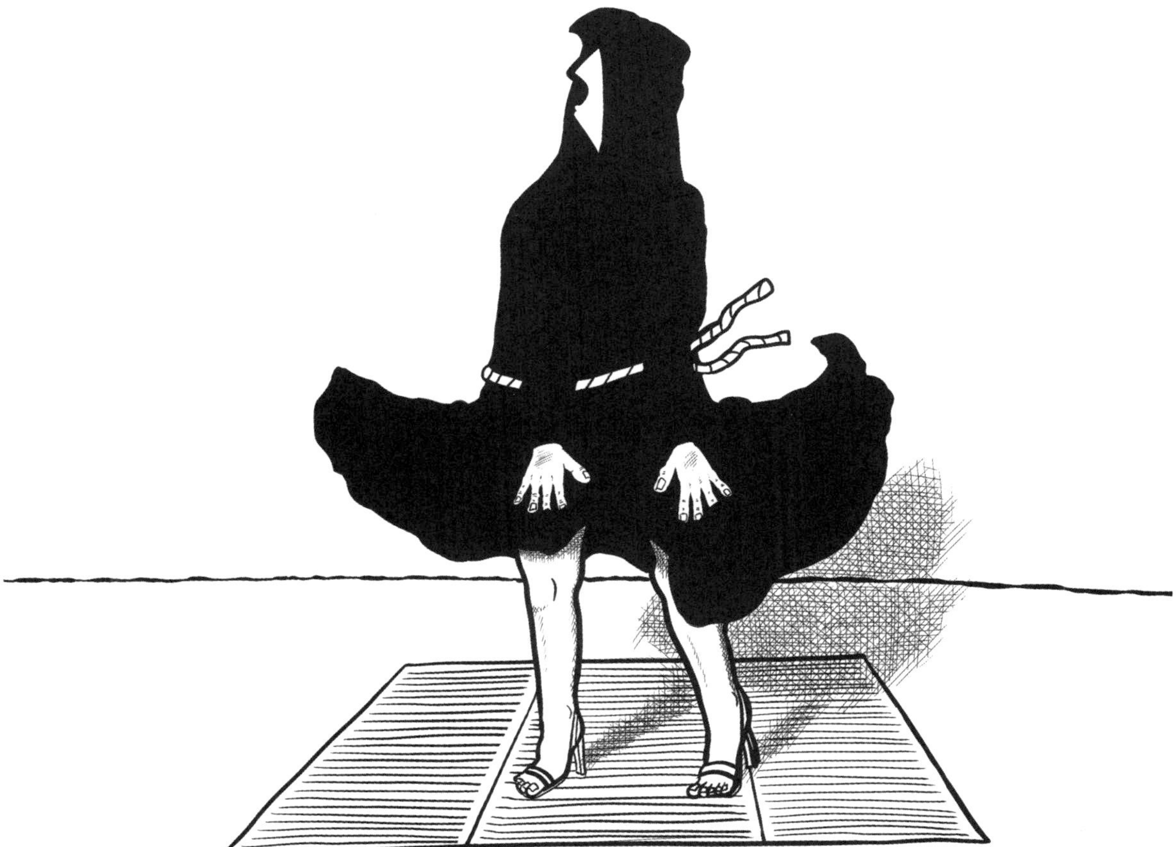

MARILYN MONKROE

IT WAS BROTHER OSWALD WHO FIRST CAME UP
WITH THE IDEA OF SPONSORSHIP

BROTHER JEREMY'S HUMILITY MADE HIM WORLD FAMOUS

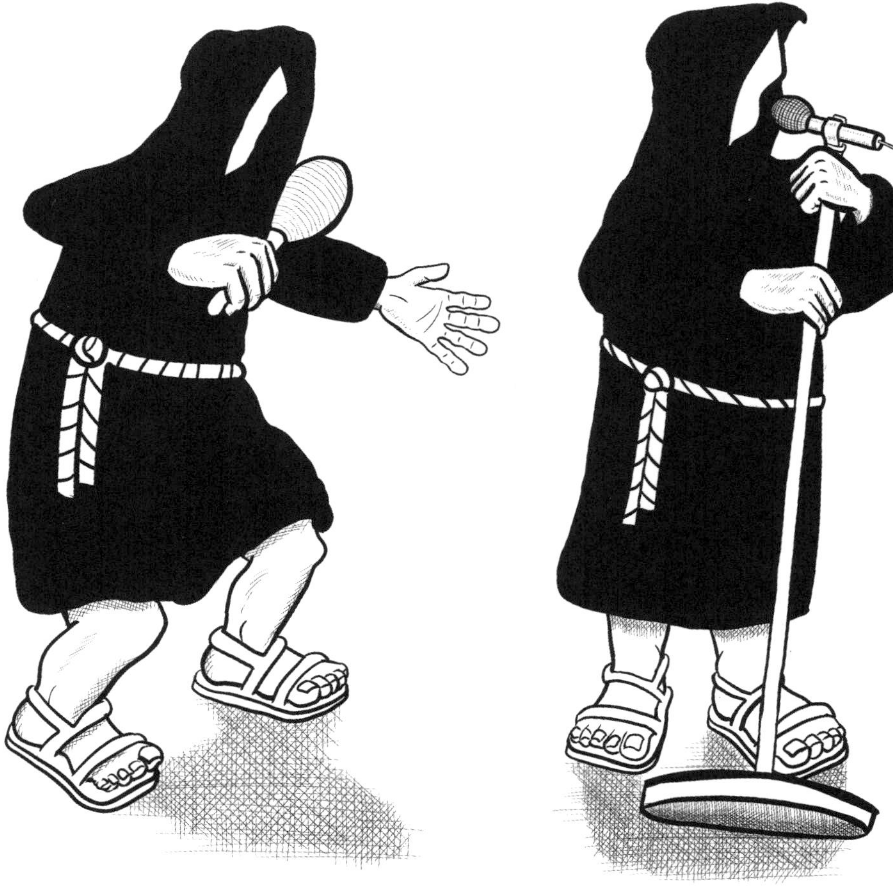

THE HAPPY MONKDAYS

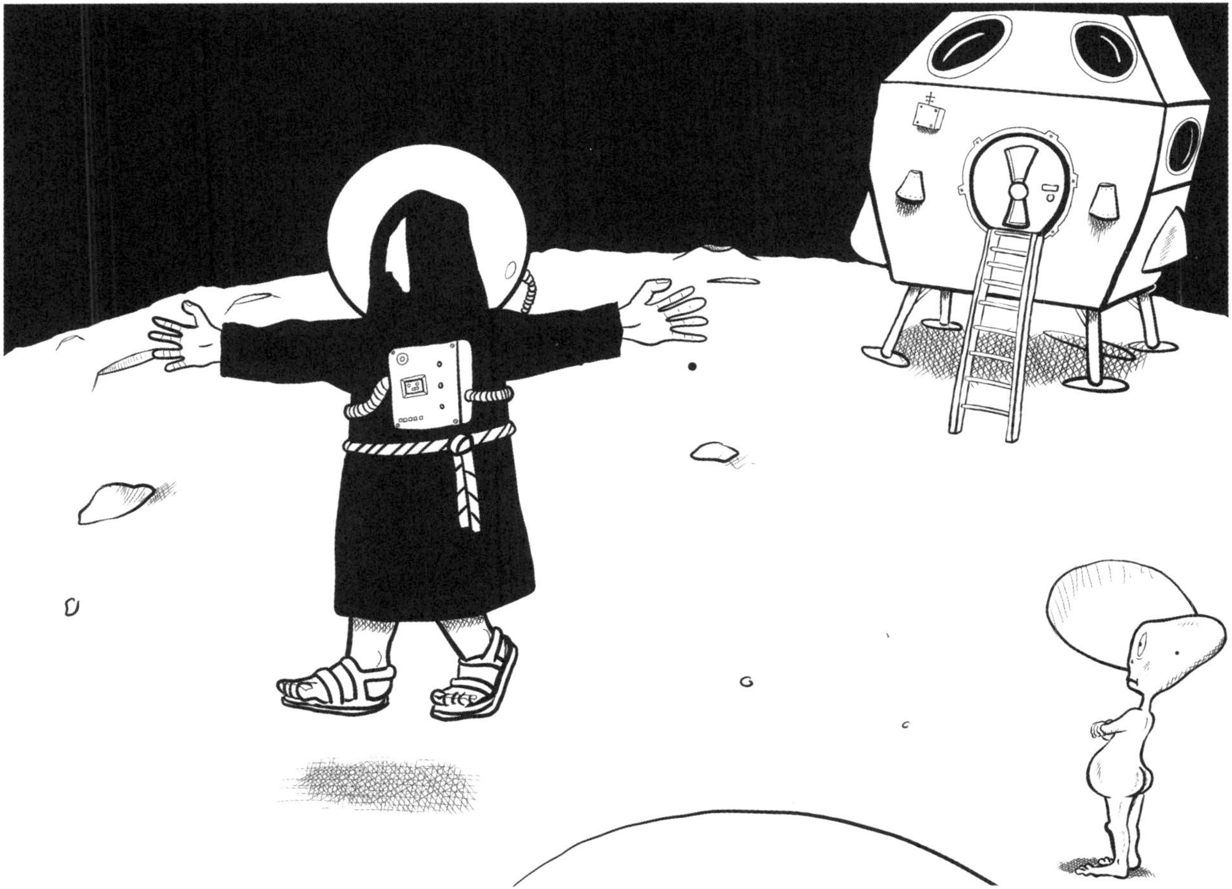

A MOONK

A KNOM

DAFT MONK

BROTHER DAVID HAD DRAWN TOO MANY MONK CARTOONS